Quotable
AUSTEN

QUOTABLE AUSTEN

An Hachette UK Company
www.hachette.co.uk

Summersdale Publishers
Part of Octopus Publishing Group Limited
Carmelite House
50 Victoria Embankment
LONDON
EC4Y 0DZ
UK

www.summersdale.com

The authorized representative in the EEA is Hachette Ireland, 8 Castlecourt Centre, Dublin 15, D15 XTP3, Ireland (email: info@hbgi.ie)

Printed and bound in China

ISBN: 978-1-83799-643-8

This FSC® label means that materials used for the product have been responsibly sourced

MIX
Paper | Supporting responsible forestry
FSC® C016973

Substantial discounts on bulk quantities of Summersdale books are available to corporations, professional associations and other organizations. For details contact general enquiries: telephone: +44 (0) 1243 771107 or email: enquiries@summersdale.com.

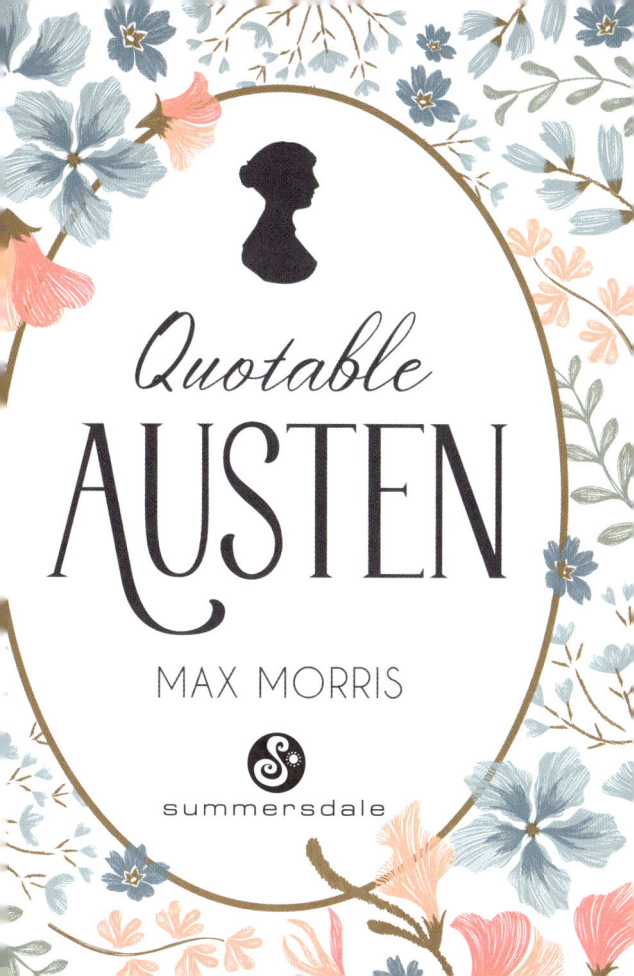

Quotable
AUSTEN

MAX MORRIS

summersdale

CONTENTS

MATTERS
OF THE
HEART

'You must allow me to tell you how ardently I admire and love you.'

FITZWILLIAM DARCY TO ELIZABETH BENNET, *PRIDE AND PREJUDICE*

'What a strange
thing love is!'

EMMA WOODHOUSE, *EMMA*

It requires uncommon
steadiness of reason to resist
the attraction of being
called the most charming
girl in the world.

NORTHANGER ABBEY

'I have come to feel for you a passionate admiration and regard, which despite all my struggles, has overcome every rational objection.'

FITZWILLIAM DARCY TO ELIZABETH BENNET, *PRIDE AND PREJUDICE*

'You really have done your hair in a more heavenly style than ever; you mischievous creature, do you want to attract everybody? I assure you, my brother is quite in love with you already.'

ISABELLA THORPE TO CATHERINE MORLAND, *NORTHANGER ABBEY*

'I suppose
there may be
a hundred different
ways of being in love.'

EMMA WOODHOUSE, *EMMA*

The happiness…
was such as he had
probably never
felt before; and he
expressed himself
on the occasion
as sensibly and as
warmly as a man
violently in love can
be supposed to do.

ON FITZWILLIAM DARCY,
PRIDE AND PREJUDICE

What could be more encouraging to a man who had her love in view?

ON FANNY PRICE,
MANSFIELD PARK

'It is such a happiness when good people get together – and they always do.'

MISS BATES, *EMMA*

'It is settled between us already, that we are to be the happiest couple in the world.'

ELIZABETH BENNET,
PRIDE AND PREJUDICE

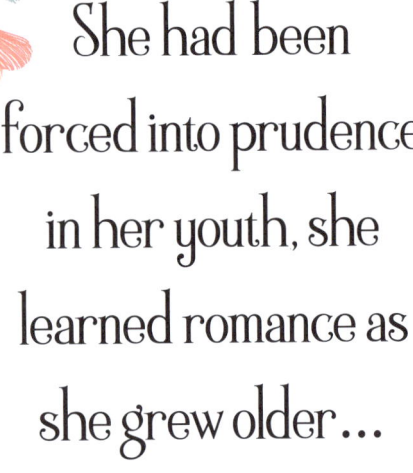

She had been
forced into prudence
in her youth, she
learned romance as
she grew older…

PERSUASION

The very first moment I beheld him, my heart was irrevocably gone.

LOVE AND FREINDSHIP [sic]

'I think you are in a very great
danger of making him as much
in love with you as ever.'

ELIZABETH BENNET,
PRIDE AND PREJUDICE

*He perfectly agreed
with her… Emma felt
herself so well acquainted
with him, that she could
hardly believe it to be only
their second meeting.*

EMMA

'I am really delighted with him; he is full as handsome… and with such open, good-humoured countenance that one cannot help loving him at first sight.'

ALICIA JOHNSON ON
MR DE COURCY, *LADY SUSAN*

'That is the only kind of love I would give a farthing for – There is some sense in being in love at first sight.'

LAURA, *LOVE AND FREINDSHIP* [*sic*]

'*Warmth and tenderness of heart, with an affectionate, open manner, will beat all the cleverness of head in the world, for attraction: I am sure it will.*'

EMMA WOODHOUSE, *EMMA*

When he was present she had no eyes for anyone else. Everything he did was right. Everything he said was clever.

ON JOHN WILLOUGHBY AND MARIANNE DASHWOOD, *SENSE AND SENSIBILITY*

'You pierce my soul. I am
half agony, half hope...
I have loved none but you.'

**CAPTAIN FREDERICK WENTWORTH TO
ANNE ELLIOT, *PERSUASION***

'At his own ball he offended two or three young ladies, by not asking them to dance; and I spoke to him twice myself, without receiving an answer. Could there be finer symptoms? Is not general incivility the very essence of love?'

ELIZABETH BENNET ON MR BINGLEY,
PRIDE AND PREJUDICE

'I never in my life saw a man more intent on being agreeable than Mr Elton… With men he can be rational and unaffected, but when he has ladies to please, every feature works.'

JOHN KNIGHTLEY, *EMMA*

LOVE'S
DISAPPOINTMENTS

Friendship is certainly the finest balm for the pangs of disappointed love.

NORTHANGER ABBEY

Nothing can compare to the misery of being bound to one, and preferring another.

LETTER TO FANNY KNIGHT

*There certainly are
not so many men of large
fortune in the world, as
there are pretty women
to deserve them.*

MANSFIELD PARK

There was one gentleman… a very good-looking young man, who, I was told, wanted very much to be introduced to me, but as he did not want it quite enough to take much trouble in effecting it, we never could bring it about.

LETTER TO CASSANDRA

You will in the course of the next two or three years meet with somebody more generally unexceptionable than anyone you have yet known, who will love you as warmly as possible, and who will so completely attract you that you will feel you never really loved before.

LETTER TO FANNY KNIGHT

'That would be the greatest misfortune of all! – To find a man agreeable whom one is determined to hate!'

ELIZABETH BENNET,
PRIDE AND PREJUDICE

No young lady can be justified
in falling in love before the
gentleman's love is declared,
it must be very improper
that a lady should dream
of a gentleman before the
gentleman is first known
to have dreamt of her.

NORTHANGER ABBEY

'I must therefore conclude that you are not serious in your rejection of me, I shall choose to attribute it to your wish of increasing my love by suspense, according to the usual practice of elegant females.'

WILLIAM COLLINS,
PRIDE AND PREJUDICE

'Man is more robust than woman, but he is not longer lived; which exactly explains my view of the nature of their attachments.'

ANNE ELLIOT, *PERSUASION*

'The more I
know of the world,
the more I am convinced
that I shall never see a man
whom I can really love.
I require so much!'

MARIANNE DASHWOOD,
SENSE AND SENSIBILITY

With such a husband,
her misery was
considered certain.

ON MR WICKHAM AND LYDIA BENNET,
PRIDE AND PREJUDICE

'There is safety in reserve,
but no attraction. One cannot
love a reserved person.'

FRANK CHURCHILL, *EMMA*

It would be mortifying to the feelings of many ladies, could they be made to understand how little the heart of man is affected by what is costly or new in their attire.

NORTHANGER ABBEY

'I had not known you a month before I felt that you were the last man in the world whom I could ever be prevailed on to marry.'

ELIZABETH BENNET
TO FITZWILLIAM DARCY,
PRIDE AND PREJUDICE

There could have been no two hearts so open, no tastes so similar, no feelings so in unison, no countenances so beloved. Now they were as strangers; nay, worse than strangers, for they could never become acquainted. It was a perpetual estrangement.

ON CAPTAIN FREDERICK WENTWORTH AND ANNE ELLIOT, *PERSUASION*

'The course of
true love never did run
smooth – A Hartfield
edition of Shakespeare
would have a long note
on that passage.'

EMMA WOODHOUSE, *EMMA*

HEALTH
AND
HAPPINESS

'But then, if one scheme of happiness fails, human nature turns to another; if the first calculation is wrong, we make a second better: we find comfort somewhere.'

MRS GRANT, MANSFIELD PARK

I bought some Japan ink… and next week shall begin my operations on my hat, on which you know my principal hopes of happiness depend.

LETTER TO CASSANDRA

Elizabeth continued her walk alone, crossing field after field at a quick pace, jumping over stiles and springing over puddles… finding herself at last within view of the house, with weary ankles, dirty stockings, and a face glowing with the warmth of exercise.

PRIDE AND PREJUDICE

'I am very sorry to hear, Miss Fairfax, of your being out this morning in the rain. Young ladies should take care of themselves. Young ladies are delicate plants. They should take care of their health and their complexion.'

MR WOODHOUSE, EMMA

Had not Elinor, in the sad countenance of her sister, seen a check to all mirth, she could have been entertained by Mrs Jennings's endeavours to cure a disappointment in love, by a variety of sweetmeats and olives, and a good fire.

SENSE AND SENSIBILITY

I continue quite well; in proof of which I have bathed again this morning. It was absolutely necessary that I should have the little fever and indisposition which I had: it has been all the fashion this week in Lyme.

LETTER TO CASSANDRA

A general spirit of ease and enjoyment seemed diffused, and they all stood about and talked and laughed, and every moment had its pleasure and its hope.

MANSFIELD PARK

'Miss Eliza Bennet, let me persuade you to follow my example, and take a turn about the room. I assure you it is very refreshing after sitting so long in one attitude.'

MISS BINGLEY, *PRIDE AND PREJUDICE*

One fatal swoon has
cost me my Life...
Beware of swoons...

LOVE AND FREINDSHIP [sic]

'But now you love a hyacinth. So much the better. You have gained a new source of enjoyment, and it is well to have as many holds upon happiness as possible.'

HENRY TILNEY, *NORTHANGER ABBEY*

'You take delight in vexing me. You have no compassion for my poor nerves.'

'You mistake me, my dear. I have a high respect for your nerves. They are my old friends. I have heard you mention them with consideration these last twenty years at least.'

MRS AND MR BENNET,
PRIDE AND PREJUDICE

GOOD
MANNERS

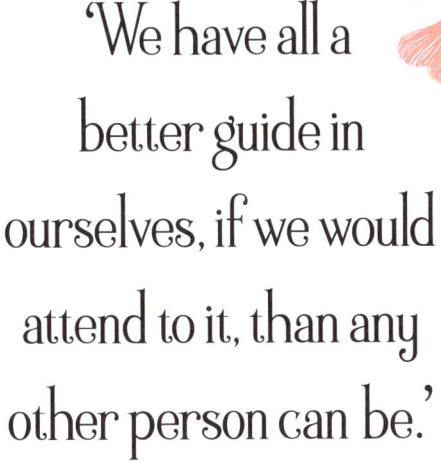

'We have all a better guide in ourselves, if we would attend to it, than any other person can be.'

FANNY PRICE, *MANSFIELD PARK*

I do not want people to be very agreeable, as it saves me the trouble of liking them a great deal.

LETTER TO CASSANDRA

'Mr Wickham is blessed
with such happy manners
as may ensure his making
friends – whether he may be
equally capable of retaining
them, is less certain.'

FITZWILLIAM DARCY,
PRIDE AND PREJUDICE

'I have a great opinion of her. Whenever I see her, she always curtseys and asks me how I do, in a very pretty manner.'

MR WOODHOUSE ON HANNAH THE HOUSEMAID, *EMMA*

She had a cultivated mind, and was, generally speaking, rational and consistent; but she had prejudices on the side of ancestry; she had a value for rank and consequence, which blinded her a little to the faults of those who possessed them.

ON LADY RUSSELL,
PERSUASION

'He is just what a young man ought to be,' said she, 'sensible, good-humoured, lively; and I never saw such happy manners! — so much ease, with such perfect good breeding!'

JANE BENNET ON MR BINGLEY,
PRIDE AND PREJUDICE

He was not an ill-disposed young man, unless to be rather cold-hearted and rather selfish is to be ill-disposed: but he was, in general, well respected; for he conducted himself with propriety in the discharge of his ordinary duties.

ON JOHN DASHWOOD,
SENSE AND SENSIBILITY

THE ARTS

'What a charming amusement for young people this is, Mr Darcy! There is nothing like dancing after all. I consider it as one of the first refinements of polished society.'

SIR WILLIAM LUCAS,
PRIDE AND PREJUDICE

It was a splendid sight, and she began, for the first time that evening, to feel herself at a ball.

ON CATHERINE MORLAND, *NORTHANGER ABBEY*

Nothing could
be more delightful!
To be fond of dancing
was a certain step
towards falling in love.

PRIDE AND PREJUDICE

There were twenty dances,
and I danced them all,
and without any fatigue.

LETTER TO CASSANDRA

'I am much mistaken if there are not some among us to whom a ball would be rather a punishment than a pleasure.'

CAROLINE BINGLEY,
PRIDE AND PREJUDICE

'But… to be quite honest, I do not think I can live without something of a musical society. I condition for nothing else, but without music, life would be a blank to me.'

EMMA WOODHOUSE, *EMMA*

'I declare after all there is no enjoyment like reading! How much sooner one tires of any thing than of a book!'

MISS BINGLEY, *PRIDE AND PREJUDICE*

Because they were fond of reading, she fancied them satirical: perhaps without exactly knowing what it was to be satirical; but that did not signify.

LADY MIDDLETON'S OPINION OF
ELINOR AND MARIANNE DASHWOOD,
SENSE AND SENSIBILITY

'There is a fine old saying, which everybody here is of course familiar with: "Keep your breath to cool your porridge"; and I shall keep mine to swell my song.'

ELIZABETH BENNET,
PRIDE AND PREJUDICE

The truth was that Sir Edward, whom circumstances had confined very much to one spot, had read more sentimental novels than agreed with him.

SANDITON

'The person, be it gentleman or lady, who has not pleasure in a good novel, must be intolerably stupid.'

'I must have my share in the conversation if you are speaking of music. There are few people in England, I suppose, who have more true enjoyment of music than myself, or a better natural taste.'

LADY CATHERINE DE BOURGH,
PRIDE AND PREJUDICE

'But it would have broke MY heart, had I loved him, to hear him read with so little sensibility.'

MARIANNE DASHWOOD ON EDWARD FERRARS, *SENSE AND SENSIBILITY*

I could not sit seriously down to write a serious romance under any other motive than to save my life.

LETTER TO JAMES STANIER CLARKE

Provided that nothing like useful knowledge could be gained from them, provided they were all story and no reflection, she had never any objection to books at all.

ON CATHERINE MORLAND,
NORTHANGER ABBEY

'And books! –
Thomson, Cowper,
Scott… she would buy
up every copy, I believe,
to prevent their falling
into unworthy hands;
and she would have
every book that tells
her how to admire an
old twisted tree. Should
not you, Marianne?'

EDWARD FERRARS,
SENSE AND SENSIBILITY

'Oh! I am delighted with the book! I should like to spend my whole life in reading it.'

CATHERINE MORLAND,
NORTHANGER ABBEY

CONVERSATION

'I certainly have not the talent which some people possess,' said Darcy, 'of conversing easily with those I have never seen before. I cannot catch their tone of conversation, or appear interested in their concerns, as I often see done.'

PRIDE AND PREJUDICE

'My idea of good company, Mr Elliot, is the company of clever, well-informed people, who have a great deal of conversation; that is what I call good company.'

'You are mistaken,' said he gently, 'that is not good company, that is the best.'

ANNE AND MR ELLIOT, *PERSUASION*

She was in gay spirits, and would have prolonged the conversation, wanting to hear the particulars of his suspicions, every look described, and all the wheres and hows of a circumstance which highly entertained her: but his gaiety did not meet hers.

ON EMMA WOODHOUSE AND
MR KNIGHTLEY, *EMMA*

Mrs Allen was… never satisfied with the day unless she spent the chief of it by the side of Mrs Thorpe, in what they called conversation, but in which there was scarcely ever any exchange of opinion, and not often any resemblance of subject.

NORTHANGER ABBEY

'For the advantage of SOME, conversation ought to be so arranged as that they may have the trouble of saying as little as possible.'

ELIZABETH BENNET,
PRIDE AND PREJUDICE

'My idea of him is, that he can adapt his conversation to the taste of every body, and has the power as well as the wish of being universally agreeable.'

EMMA WOODHOUSE ON
FRANK CHURCHILL, *EMMA*

I have subdued
him entirely by
sentiment and serious
conversation, and
made him, I may
venture to say, at
least half in love
with me, without
the semblance of the
most commonplace
flirtation.

LADY SUSAN

Marianne was silent; it was impossible for her to say what she did not feel, however trivial the occasion; and upon Elinor therefore the whole task of telling lies when politeness required it, always fell.

SENSE AND SENSIBILITY

Their conversation turned upon those subjects, of which the free discussion has generally much to do in perfecting a sudden intimacy between two young ladies: such as dress, balls, flirtations, and quizzes.

NORTHANGER ABBEY

'Here is a young man wishing to pay his addresses to you, with everything to recommend him: not merely situation in life, fortune, and character, but with more than common agreeableness, with address and conversation pleasing to everybody.'

SIR THOMAS BERTRAM ON HENRY CRAWFORD, *MANSFIELD PARK*

CLASS
AND
WEALTH

'If they had uncles enough to fill all Cheapside,' cried Bingley, 'it would not make them one jot less agreeable.'

'But it must very materially lessen their chance of marrying men of any consideration in the world,' replied Darcy.

PRIDE AND PREJUDICE

It would be an excellent
match, for he was rich,
and she was handsome.

SENSE AND SENSIBILITY

'He is a gentleman, and I am a gentleman's daughter. So far we are equal.'

ELIZABETH BENNET,
PRIDE AND PREJUDICE

'What have wealth or grandeur
to do with happiness?'

'Grandeur has but little,'
said Elinor, 'but wealth
has much to do with it.'

MARIANNE AND ELINOR DASHWOOD,
SENSE AND SENSIBILITY

'A large income
is the best recipe
for happiness I
ever heard of.'

MARY CRAWFORD, *MANSFIELD PARK*

'The world is blinded by his fortune and consequence, or frightened by his high and imposing manners, and sees him only as he chooses to be seen.'

MR WICKHAM ON FITZWILLIAM DARCY,
PRIDE AND PREJUDICE

'She is poor; she has sunk from the comforts she was born to; and, if she live to old age, must probably sink more. Her situation should secure your compassion.'

MR KNIGHTLEY ON MISS BATES, *EMMA*

'The interest of two thousand pounds — how can a man live on it!... I cannot picture to myself a more wretched condition.'

JOHN DASHWOOD,
SENSE AND SENSIBILITY

Harriet's parentage
became known.
She proved to be
the daughter of a
tradesman, rich
enough to afford
her the comfortable
maintenance which
had ever been hers,
and decent enough to
have always wished
for concealment.

EMMA

104

'If a smart young colonel, with
five or six thousand a year,
should want one of my girls
I shall not say nay to him.'

MRS BENNET, *PRIDE AND PREJUDICE*

Mrs Morland knew so little of lords and baronets, that she entertained no notion of their general mischievousness, and was wholly unsuspicious of danger to her daughter from their machinations.

NORTHANGER ABBEY

The dinner was a grand one, the servants were numerous, and every thing bespoke the Mistress's inclination for show, and the Master's ability to support it.

SENSE AND SENSIBILITY

Mary was in a state of mind to rejoice in a connexion with the Bertram family, and to be not displeased with her brother's marrying a little beneath him.

MANSFIELD PARK

WICKED
WIT

People always
live forever when
there is an annuity
to be paid them.

SENSE AND SENSIBILITY

Another stupid party last night; perhaps if larger they might be less intolerable, but here there were only just enough to make one card-table, with six people to look on and talk nonsense to each other.

LETTER TO CASSANDRA

'One cannot be always laughing at a man without now and then stumbling on something witty.'

ELIZABETH BENNET,
PRIDE AND PREJUDICE

Miss Debary, Susan and Sally…
made their appearance, and
I was as civil to them as their
bad breath would allow me.

LETTER TO CASSANDRA

Wisdom is better than wit, and in the long run will certainly have the laugh on her side.

LETTER TO FANNY KNIGHT

'Brandon is just the kind of man,' said Willoughby one day, when they were talking of him together, 'whom everybody speaks well of, and nobody cares about; whom all are delighted to see, and nobody remembers to talk to.'

JOHN WILLOUGHBY TO ELINOR AND MARIANNE DASHWOOD, *SENSE AND SENSIBILITY*

I will not say that your mulberry-trees are dead, but I am afraid they are not alive.

LETTER TO CASSANDRA

Pictures of perfection
make me sick
and wicked.

LETTER TO FANNY KNIGHT

Lady Middleton was
more agreeable than
her mother, only in
being more silent.

SENSE AND SENSIBILITY

There certainly were a dreadful multitude of ugly women in Bath; and as for the men! they were infinitely worse.

PERSUASION

'A clergyman has nothing to do but be slovenly and selfish; read the newspaper, watch the weather, and quarrel with his wife. His curate does all the work and the business of his own life is to dine.'

MISS CRAWFORD, *MANSFIELD PARK*

Mr Richard Harvey is going to be married; but as it is a great secret and only known to half the neighbourhood, you must not mention it.

LETTER TO CASSANDRA

John Dashwood
had not much to say
for himself that was
worth hearing, and
his wife had still less.

SENSE AND SENSIBILITY

Mrs Portman is not much admired in Dorsetshire; the good-natured world as usual extolled her beauty so highly that all the neighbourhood have had the pleasure of being disappointed.

LETTER TO CASSANDRA

'For what do we live,
but to make sport for our
neighbours, and laugh
at them in our turn?'

MR BENNET, *PRIDE AND PREJUDICE*

'A woman is not to marry a man merely because she is asked, or because he is attached to her, and can write a tolerable letter.'

EMMA WOODHOUSE, *EMMA*

He has but one fault,
which time will, I trust,
entirely remove — it is
that his morning coat is
a great deal too light.

LETTER TO CASSANDRA

It may be possible to
do without dancing
entirely. Instances
have been known of
young people passing
many, many months
successively, without
being at any ball
of any description,
and no material
injury accrue either
to body or mind.

EMMA

How little of permanent
happiness could belong
to a couple who were
only brought together
because their passions were
stronger than their virtue.

PRIDE AND PREJUDICE

Had he married a more amiable woman, he might have been made still more respectable than he was: he might even have been made amiable himself.

ON JOHN DASHWOOD,
SENSE AND SENSIBILITY

We met a Gentleman in a Buggy, who on minute examination turned out to be Dr Hall — and Dr Hall in such very deep mourning that either his Mother, his Wife, or himself must be dead.

LETTER TO CASSANDRA

'I do suspect that he is
not really necessary
to my happiness. So
much the better.'

His temper might perhaps be a little soured by finding, like many others of his sex, that through some unaccountable bias in favour of beauty, he was the husband of a very silly woman.

SENSE AND SENSIBILITY

I would rather
be a teacher at a
school (and I can
think of nothing
worse) than marry
a man I did not like.

EMMA WATSON, *THE WATSONS*

'If he is satisfied with only regretting me, when he might have obtained my affections and hand, I shall soon cease to regret him at all.'

ELIZABETH BENNET,
PRIDE AND PREJUDICE

You deserve a longer letter than this; but it is my unhappy fate seldom to treat people so well as they deserve.

LETTER TO CASSANDRA

'I would rather
work for my bread
than marry him.'

'Seven years would be insufficient to make some people acquainted with each other, and seven days are more than enough for others.'

MARIANNE DASHWOOD,
SENSE AND SENSIBILITY

'If this man had not twelve thousand a year, he would be a very stupid fellow.'

EDMUND BERTRAM ON MR RUSHWORTH, *MANSFIELD PARK*

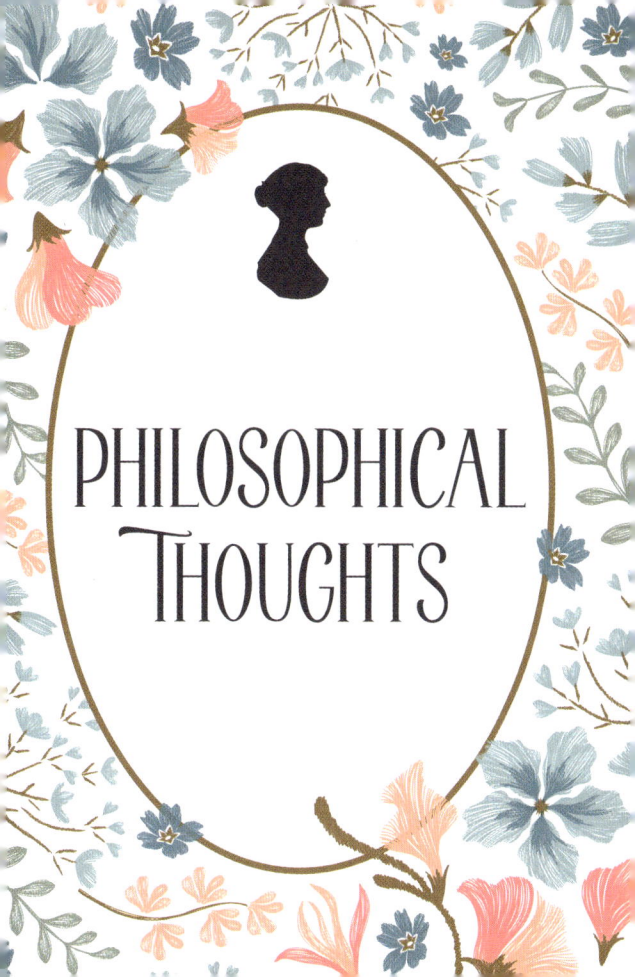

PHILOSOPHICAL
THOUGHTS

It is a truth
universally acknowledged,
that a single man in
possession of a good
fortune must be in
want of a wife.

PRIDE AND PREJUDICE

'Why did we wait for any thing? – why not seize the pleasure at once? – How often is happiness destroyed by preparation, foolish preparation!'

MR KNIGHTLEY, *EMMA*

Nobody minds having
what is too good for them.

MANSFIELD PARK

'There is something so amiable in the prejudices of a young mind, that one is sorry to see them give way to the reception of more general opinions.'

COLONEL BRANDON,
SENSE AND SENSIBILITY

'It was, perhaps, one of those cases in which advice is good or bad only as the event decides.'

ANNE ELLIOT, *PERSUASION*

Besides, I cannot help thinking that it is more natural to have flowers grow out of the head than fruit.

LETTER TO CASSANDRA

A woman, especially if she have the misfortune of knowing anything, should conceal it as well as she can.

NORTHANGER ABBEY

'Men are much
more philosophic
on the subject of
beauty than they are
generally supposed;
till they do fall in love
with well-informed
minds instead of
handsome faces.'

EMMA WOODHOUSE,
EMMA

'I speak what appears to me the general opinion; and where an opinion is general, it is usually correct.'

FANNY PRICE, *MANSFIELD PARK*

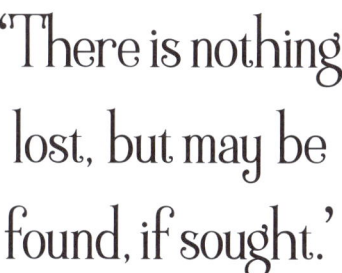

'There is nothing lost, but may be found, if sought.'

COLONEL BRANDON
(QUOTING FROM SPENCER'S
THE FAERIE QUEEN),
SENSE AND SENSIBILITY

'If a woman doubts as to whether she should accept a man or not, she certainly ought to refuse him.'

EMMA WOODHOUSE, *EMMA*

To look almost pretty is an acquisition of higher delight to a girl who has been looking plain for the first fifteen years of her life than a beauty from her cradle can ever receive.

NORTHANGER ABBEY

'Know your own happiness. You want for nothing but patience – or give it a more fascinating name: call it hope.'

MRS DASHWOOD,
SENSE AND SENSIBILITY

How quick come the reasons for approving what we like!

PERSUASION

Angry people are
not always wise.

PRIDE AND PREJUDICE

'*Selfishness must always be forgiven, you know, because there is no hope of a cure.*'

MISS CRAWFORD, *MANSFIELD PARK*

'One half of the world cannot understand the pleasures of the other.'

EMMA WOODHOUSE, *EMMA*

'Sometimes one is guided by what other people say of them, without giving oneself time to deliberate and judge.'

ELINOR DASHWOOD,
SENSE AND SENSIBILITY

'One man's ways may be as good as another's, but we all like our own best.'

ADMIRAL CROFT, *PERSUASION*

Let other pens dwell on guilt and misery. I quit such odious subjects as soon as I can.

MANSFIELD PARK

Have you enjoyed this book?

If so, find us on Facebook at
Summersdale Publishers, on Twitter/X
at **@Summersdale** and on Instagram and
TikTok at **@summersdalebooks** and get in
touch. We'd love to hear from you!

www.summersdale.com